TABLE OF CONTENTS

HOW THE CABBAGE CAME TO BE

Have you ever wished to fly? Have you ever dreamt of having wings? If you have, listen to this story about a cabbage who dreamt such a dream. If you have not, you might still listen to this story because you too, may dream an impossible dream which might one day come true. And then you will remember the tale of the cabbage who wished to have wings.

In the beginning, this cabbage was just a seedling deep in the moist soil, who could neither feel, nor hear nor see. And then the miracle of life happened in the dark womb of the earth. The seedling sprouted a little shoot. And the little shoot started turning into a baby cabbage, which started to see despite the darkness, to hear despite the silence, and above all to think and to feel.

Can cabbages think and feel, see and hear? How can they hear if we cannot see their ears or see if we cannot see their eyes? The answer is that though we have eyes we often do not see what is to be seen, and though we have ears often do not hear what is to be heard.

When we look at cabbages, all we see are green leaves, and nothing else. In fact, if our eyes could see better, we would see that in each one of their outer leaves, they have as many eyes, ears and noses as there are stars in the sky, which means that they can see, smell and hear far better than humans.

Cabbages are strange in another way, also, for they are neither only boy nor only girl, but a mixture of both. The more girlish half of our cabbage was called Sheehee and the more boyish, Heeshee. They were separate, yet one, and the one was the cabbage.

Their very first feeling when they were merely two parts of a shoot was that of sleeping in sweet entanglement, or to put it more simply, gently joined to each other in their cabbage cradle. Gradually, the shoot grew. As it grew, the first thoughts started floating from the two halves of its sleepy brain, thoughts which one half had to share with the other half.

"I wonder if we shall go on sleeping for evermore," Heeshee yawned.

"I would not mind that at all," Sheehee replied. "I had a lovely dream that one day we found ourselves outside the darkness of the earth, and there was an extraordinary world full of all sorts of wonderful things! I feel so excited by what is going to happen to us…"

"I don't feel at all excited," Heeshee moaned. "I had a nightmare that we were above the earth in the vast and cold outside, and that all sorts of monsters were coming to eat us. It sent a shiver down to the very tips of my roots! I think I would rather stay just as we are, safely sleeping in the bosom of the soil. So cosy! So safe!"

"Hush! Listen!" Sheehee interrupted. "Did you hear?"

MONSTERS OF THE EARTH

Heeshee listened to the midnight soil and heard sinister sounds in the darkness around: beasts creeping and crawling and, worse still, chewing and munching... And nothing is more terrifying for the little shoot of a cabbage, than to feel that all around them the cabbage eating monsters are closing in on you, especially knowing that as your roots are held in the tight grip of the earth, there is no way of escape.

Closer and closer grew the sounds. Suddenly something slithered just by them: a long and fat, pink and slimy: a worm...

"Yuck! What a disgusting beast!" Heeshee gulped.
"At least it did not eat us!" said Sheehee. "Let's hope all those other creatures we can hear are as harmless as that worm."

In the next few days as the little cabbage drew closer to the surface of the earth lots of strange little monsters passed them by: beetles, earwigs, centipedes, millipedes, and other weird and wonderful creatures. They were far too busy to pester, let alone eat the growing shoots of cabbages. So, the two halves of the baby cabbage slept, dreamt and waited. The one worrying, the other hoping.

A WORLD OF WONDER

At long last, the great moment came. That moment of squeezing out of the earth and peeping for the very first time at the enormous world around, no longer hugged on all sides by black soil. Though they were still rooted in it, they had suddenly sprouted leaves, which meant that now they could see and hear as they had never seen or heard before. And what a delicious feeling that was! They felt fresh air and crystal droplets of dew, for dawn was about to break. From the darkness grew the first glimmer of light and the sweet singing of a spring morning bursting into life everywhere.

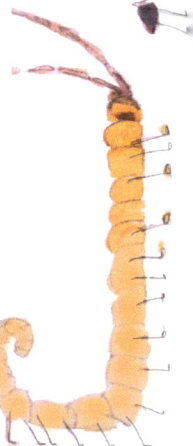

For the first time, the little cabbage felt part of a world infinitely mysterious and beautiful. And if that spring morning was bursting with life, so too, both halves of the little cabbage were bursting with bliss, so much so that their leaves were covered with tears. But maybe that was the dew, or maybe with cabbages there is no difference between raindrops, dew and tears…

They could hear songs raining down upon their leaves from everywhere. At first they thought it must be the singing of the awakening of the of light, but then gazing up in wonder at the trees they saw that these songs were pouring out of the beaks of all kinds of birds: blackbirds and thrushes, wrens and robins, as well as many other birds. Few sounds are more thrilling than the magical interweaving of the dawn chorus! But there was one sound which tickled the cabbage's leaves and made them curl into what looked like a smile: that of a cuckoo calling "Cuckoo! Cuckoo!"

The other exciting event of that dawn was that other little cabbages had popped their leafy heads out at the same time, each one of them feeling the same excitement at seeing one another at last and at seeing the world above which had fed into their dreams and nightmares for so long in the soil's timeless night.

MYSTERIES FIRST SEEN AND FEARED

"Look at that golden ball of fire staring at us!" cried one. "I hope it is not going to burn us!"

"Look at all the blue earth above us!" cried another. "I hope it won't crush us!"

"And look at those shapes of white and grey floating across the blue earth!" whispered yet another. "I hope they're not going to eat us!"

"How stupid you all are!" cackled a magpie who was hopping and pecking nearby. "What you call a golden ball of fire is the sun without which we cannot live, and what you call the blue earth is the sky. The grey and white shapes are the clouds, without which there is no rain, and without which you would never have grown!"

Apart from the sun and the sky and the clouds, what really astonished the cabbages were the most gigantic cabbages on extraordinarily long stalks rising all around them high into the sky and swaying in a strange kind of dance, their leaves fresh and sparkling in the early spring sun, whispering in the wind. Well, for you and me, they did not look anything like cabbages, but then cabbages see the world in a very different way, so what you and I know as trees, they saw as gigantic cabbages. And echoing amongst those trees, cutting through all the other sounds, came the dramatic drumming of a woodpecker's beak beating on a tree trunk.

Besides the trees there were all kinds of other surprises that you and I take for granted: emerald grass, bushes and all sorts of flowers, like bluebells deep in the beech wood, and along its fringes the last of the yellow daffodils and primroses, white narcissi and even the first of the red poppies. What a world of colour! What a feast of beauty! On that first day above the surface of the earth the cabbages became drunk with beauty! And for a while, there were no worries nor sense of lurking danger. Just delight at everything they saw in this ever changing and surprising world!

As the sun rose and the air became warm and heavy with the scent of flowers and growing plants, the cabbages listened entranced by the singing birds, the buzzing of bees and other insects, the call of crickets and a chorus of grasshoppers.

AT WAR WITH NATURE

Gradually, however, something sinister started to happen which made the cabbages' leaves curl with a mixture of fear, dread and disgust. As black clouds gather and blot out a blue sky, or storm-darkened waves of the incoming tide roll over the golden sands of a beach, so now the beautiful scents and sounds of the early morning became infected by hideous noises and foul smells.

What are those smells and noises?" they all cried in alarm. "They must surely be cabbage-eating monsters!"

The magpie, who always seemed to be dancing and pecking nearby, cackled his usual cackle before explaining:

"Those smells and noises come from machines. Machines eat silence but not cabbages."

"Machines, what are they?" the cabbages asked.

For once, the magpie stopped cackling. He even stopped hopping. He looked thoughtful, his long black tail dipping up and down before going on to explain what he thought machines were:

"Machines do all sorts of strange things, such as cutting, drilling, killing, mowing and moving…above all moving…"

The cabbages listened in open-leaved wonder. They had not the slightest idea of what all these actions were. Indeed, though they had seen birds, bees and butterflies flying, rooted as they were to the ground, they only had a hazy idea of what it meant to move or why anything should wish to move. Was it not enough just to look and listen?

"Why do machines move?" they asked. "Why don't they just stay still and enjoy BEING?"

"Dear me! How horribly boring that would be!" the dancing magpie chuckled. Just then, and only a short distance away from them, a roaring monster shot past, making the ground shake, filling the air with fumes and the cabbages with fear. No sooner had it disappeared, and the cabbages were recovering from their shock, than the silence was broken by another roar, this time from the sky above. It came from a silver, bird-like beast whose wings stuck out without flapping but who left a white scar stretching behind long after it had disappeared.

All the cabbages stared at the scar in the sky. The first time they peered at the world, it had been paradise. Now it was paradise no longer. Ugliness, destruction and danger hung

heavy in the once pure air. The machines seemed to be at war with nature. But why?

The magpie, his little black eyes glinting with malicious delight, watched the dismay etched on the cabbages' leaves, and then being a know-it-all, he could not resist showing off his knowledge:

"The first machine you saw is called a lorry, and the other one up there in the sky is an aeroplane."

"But why were they in such a hurry?" the cabbages asked. "Why were they going so fast?"

"My word! What silly questions you ask!" chortled the magpie. "The machines don't decide whether they move or not. They can't do anything without humans."

STRANGE FEATHERLESS BIRDS

"Humans?" cried the cabbages with one voice. "What on earth are they?"

"What are humans?" the magpie mimicked their question in a mocking voice.

"They're big, featherless birds! They can be all sorts of colours, like black, red, white, pink, yellow, brown. They're rather clumsy and slow but love moving fast, so they use machines, like the ones you have just seen. The smellier and the noisier the machine, the happier the human. Machines bring out the worst in humans, and humans bring out the worst in machines."

"What on earth makes you say that?" Sheehee asked, bewildered by the things the magpie said.

For a moment, the magpie cocked his head, trying to think his way through what he had just said, before continuing:

"Well, if a machine is all alone without a human, it just sleeps peacefully without disturbing the world and with no need for humans. But when a human arrives all hell breaks loose."

"Do all machines make a noise when humans are around?" Heeshee asked, trying to understand the weird world of machines.

"No, not all of them!" replied the magpie. "In fact, the ones without which humans cannot breathe, see, hear, or talk, are quite silent really. I've heard humans call them "smart phones". Without them, humans cannot live because to stay alive they need to exercise their eyes by staring at the screens, their voices by talking to them, their fingers by tapping at them. It's a clear case of symbiosis…"

"SIN what?" all the cabbages cried with one voice, baffled by this long and strange word. This time the magpie was still for a moment, something most unusual for him. He raised a wing and picked at it, before answering:

"My poor dears, you don't seem to know anything! Not surprising, I suppose, as you've only been around since this morning. Symbiosis means that humans and machines depend on each other. No machine, no human, no human, no machine."

For a while, all the cabbages were silent, buried in thought, trying to understand. The busy magpie was about to fly off when Sheehee broke the silence: "Yes, but apart from being machine-loving, featherless birds, how do they spend their lives?"

The magpie was impatient and wanted to get on with his life. But at the same time he could not help chattering, so he answered, dancing on one leg and then on the other:

"Humans: they like stealing. Not that I see anything wrong in stealing, mind you. Anyone with any sense steals. Life is all about stealing, when you come to think about it. I just love stealing birds' eggs from their nests. But, those humans, they steal absolutely everything they can lay their hands on. If they could get their hands on them, there would be no stars, sun or moon! No one is safe from humans. Nothing is safe from them. And YOU certainly are not! In fact, I saw the human being who planted you. He is waiting until you are ready for the picking. And then he will gobble you up, as he has gobbled up all the cabbages that have ever come before you…"

DARK THOUGHTS AND THE DYING OF THE LIGHT

Whereupon the magpie flew away still chattering and chortling, leaving the cabbages stunned and silent. The roots of every single one of them twisted and turned in horror. It had never entered their leafy brains that their lives were to be cut short. They had thought when they had first seen the outside world that they would go on and on, listening to birds and bees, looking at blue skies drawing pictures of clouds, and feasting on the rich soil beneath them until they became as tall as the trees around them. Maybe even larger!

The spring light suddenly lost its sparkle as black clouds rolled into the blue sky above. A heavy shower spattered raindrops on the miserable cabbages. Each one tried to imagine what a cabbage-eating human being could look like.

But then, just as suddenly, a ray of sunshine broke through the clouds and Sheehee, ever full of hope, spoke:

"We must not believe all that the magpie says, even though he is so clever and has lived so much longer than us. He said some very odd things. I don't think he can be trusted. I'm sure that everything will be all right and we shall live for evermore. It just cannot be that we shall be eaten by a featherless ogre. It would be so unfair! So pointless!"

Such was the conviction in Sheehee's voice, and such was the wish of the cabbages to hope and to live that they clutched at these words with every leaf of their beings. Besides, the black clouds had melted away, leaving in their wake a radiant spring evening. As the raindrops melted in the warm air, so did their gloom. The clouds had sailed to the horizon and now shone red and golden under the dark blue sky of the setting sun, surely confirming that the magpie had told a lie as black as its blackest feathers. And for a while, they forgot the machines and their masters.

Presently though, the sun sank behind the trees and their shadows grew long and threatening. The light started to fade. The air lost its warmth. Night was falling, and so did the mood of the cabbages, who could not understand why that wonderful world of light and colour which had made them so happy had passed away. All kinds of strange fears and fantasies took possession of them. Was the sinister darkness eating the blessed light? Or was the darkness a spell cast by the cabbage gobbling ogre who had planted them? Or were they being swallowed into a monster-infested belly of the earth?

"I don't want to be eaten by the earth!!" Heeshee sobbed, echoing the fear of some of the other cabbages. "But still less by that horrible human ogre!"

"What a silly half-cabbage, you are!" cried Sheehee. "Don't you remember how frightened you were of what would happen to us when we were no longer in the safety of the soil? And now you're afraid of going back to that very same world where once you felt so safe. Don't jump to conclusions! If we are to go back into the earth, it may all be for the best. At least the cabbage-eating ogre, if IT does indeed exist, won't eat us, and we'll be cosy down there, you and me together, two hugging halves of one happy cabbage."

Whatever the darkness, Sheehee always saw a glimmer of light. Whatever the light, Heeshee was always fearful of the coming of the night. Which one of them do you think was right? Well, just listen to what happened next.

THE EYES OF THE NIGHT

The world around our family of cabbages was wrapped in darkness, and they felt they could no longer see when suddenly one tiny eye and then another appeared in the night sky. Soon there were hundreds, thousands on thousands of silver eyes, piercing the darkness and staring down at the cabbages, while the cabbages for their part gazed up at the staring eyes of the night sky in open-leaved wonder.

As the light had faded at the end of the day, so did their fears, for they all told themselves that the eyes high up there were the eyes of all the cabbages who had lived and died, becoming alive again in the heaven above. Spellbound, the cabbages gazed deep into the deep night sky until at last, one after another, their heads drooped towards the earth, and still marvelling they fell asleep. Under that starlit night the cabbages slept the perfect sleep that only innocent, uneaten little cabbages can sleep, a sleep full of dreams fed on the beauty that they had seen and heard on their first day in the open air.

The next day, all the cabbages awoke at dawn, rubbing their sleepy leaves with delight for another day of the sounds and sights of spring, remembering only their good memories, forgetting the bad ones. Bliss was it in that dawn to be alive, but to be a young cabbage was like heaven!

THE OGRE AND THE CABBAGE EATING CATERPILLARS

The days slipped by and so did the nights, and the cabbages grew ever plumper. And that is when things started to go wrong. They saw it, ugly and terrifying: a featherless giant about which the magpie had spoken. The cabbages shuddered down to their roots. They realised it must be the cabbage-eating monster. It looked at them, made a salivary sucking sound between its yellow, hungry teeth, grinned and muttered: "They're growing nicely this year. Should be ready for the picking quite soon. They'll be really good as long as those caterpillars don't get at them!"

After that, there was not a day when IT did not come, that cabbage eating ogre, to glare and gloat. And as if that was not enough, all the cabbages became plagued by an unbearable itching feeling. And believe you me, nothing is worse than to be an itching cabbage since you cannot scratch yourself because you have no hands and no nails.

What was it that was making them itch so badly? Can you guess? Well, I had better tell you: it was a swarm of green caterpillars nibbling the cabbages' leaves.

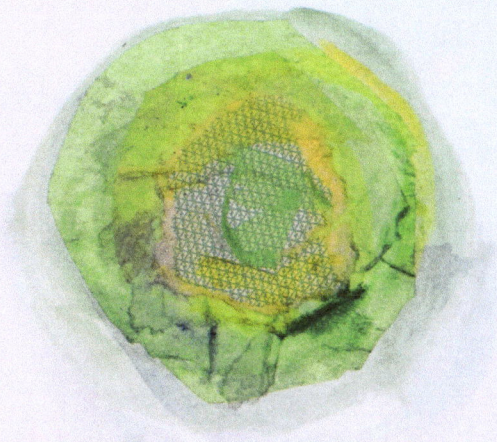

"This is awful! I can't bear it!!" Heeshee sobbed.

"Don't be such a cry-cabbage!" Sheehee said, before adding: "We'll get used to them, and once you get used to something, it's never so bad!"

"I'll never get used to it!" wailed Heeshee. "It's far worse for me than it is for you!"

"Oh yes, you will," Sheehee said gently. And as so often happened Sheehee was right. Both halves of our cabbage grew used to the caterpillars, so much so that one day Sheehee said:

"That itching has turned into a tickling, and I quite like that tickling, don't you? And anyway, I'd rather be eaten bit by little bit by these pretty green caterpillars than all at once by that disgusting cabbage-eating ogre. I quite like them, really, and I like to hear the caterpillars talking to each other, even though they always speak with their mouths full, which is rather rude."

And indeed, the caterpillars were quite talkative, discussing all sorts of things as they nibbled. One conversation in particular stuck in both parts of our cabbage's mind.

"You know," one of the caterpillars said as he chewed on a cabbage leaf, "I've heard that one day we'll have wings and fly like those birds up there, and that instead of eating cabbage, we shall fly from flower to flower…"

"What utter rot!" exclaimed one of the other caterpillars. "Once a caterpillar, always a caterpillar. I would hate to have wings and fly onto flowers. I far prefer chewing away on juicy cabbages. My only wish is to go on doing this forever and ever more."

Sheehee was quite excited at the thought that caterpillars could one day have wings and fly like birds, but maybe it was only a caterpillar dream. Heeshee, on the other hand, was convinced that the idea of a caterpillar ever having wings was indeed utter rot. How silly of Sheehee to be taken in by such rubbish!

A STRANGE DREAM

That night Sheehee had a strange dream: they had each become the wings of a bird on either side of their cabbage self and flown away from the cabbage-eating ogre just as IT was about to gobble them. Sheehee awoke. What a happy dream it had been! If only it had not been just a dream! Oh to become a pair of wings! Sheehee one wing and Heeshee the other, flying away and out of reach of the cabbage-gobbling ogre.

On the next morning Sheehee told the other cabbages about the dream. They laughed scornfully at the preposterous idea, but Heeshee did not, for Heeshee and Sheehee were two halves of the same cabbage, and each half loved the other half even more than they did themselves. They were loyal to each other even when they disagreed and knew they could

only be themselves and complete if they were joined in that one whole cabbage, each feeling fiercely protective of their other half.

One of the cabbages was particularly contemptuous and made the following pronouncement: "Cabbages can never fly. Our roots are firmly in the earth, and we're more likely to grow and fill the sky rather than fly! Or turn into the full moon! Just imagine that! A green cabbage moon sailing in the sky! Ha! Ha!"

This idea of filling the sky did not appeal to our cabbage, for whom it was an ever changing and miraculous friend. If you filled the sky, you could no longer be able to see it, and what could be sadder than no longer looking at the sky, all blue sometimes, grey at others, clouds sailing past, each drawing strange and wonderful shapes of improbable creatures and landscapes?

And all the cabbages laughed, except for the cabbage whose one half dreamt of flying, and whose other half wished to share the same dream, however impossible it might be...

A DISAPPEARANCE

The moon does strange things to the earth, and maybe it was because of the full moon that it happened; or maybe not. But happened it did. One morning our cabbage awoke and no longer felt the caterpillars tickling them, nor heard them talking to each other as they chewed. And both halves of the cabbage felt lonely, for they had grown fond of the nibbling caterpillars. The caterpillars had just melted away, like dew in the rays of the warm sun. All that could be felt were little apparently lifeless lumps here and there.

Both halves of our cabbage were most upset, convinced their caterpillars had all died of some terrible disease. How very sad! But sometimes it is when you feel most sad and lonely that suddenly something happens which changes everything and makes you smile and laugh, sometimes even dance. Not that cabbages can dance, not even our cabbage, who was the most exceptional of cabbages, for, like all cabbages, it was rooted to the earth.

Neither half of our cabbage had the least idea of what had really happened to the caterpillars, but I shall tell you a secret. Each caterpillar had turned into a chrysalis. That is to say that each had made itself a little house in which it fell asleep. And while sleeping it gradually changed from a green caterpillar into a white butterfly with one or two black dots on each wing.

And so it came to be that one fine morning when the sun had warmed the cabbages' leaves, the caterpillars who had become butterflies wriggled out of their houses and flew out in a fluttering clouds. Sheehee gazed up in open-leaved wonder. In a way Sheehee felt part of each one of those flying caterpillars, those caterpillars who had become butterflies, and who had fed on the cabbage of which Sheehee was one half and Heeshee the other half.

Sheehee felt strangely and blissfully free from those roots that anchored the cabbage to the earth. Heeshee, on the other hand, felt as rooted to the earth as ever. Which was right, I wonder? Is it better to dream and hope or is it better to doubt?

ON THE WINGS OF A DREAM

The very next day, the human being started digging up the cabbages and carting them away, leaving all the other cabbages feeling miserable, knowing that their turn would come soon and that there was no escape. And what made them feel even worse was the magpie, hopping around, pecking here and there, cackling at his own jokes, his straight tail bobbing up and down. Because the end was so near and inevitable, the cabbages felt even more poignantly the warmth of the sun, the freshness of the raindrops as they pattered on the ground, the whispering of the wind in the leaves of the trees… So many sights and sounds, so many joys!

the whispering of the wind in the leaves of the trees

And all about to end so quickly!

"What happens when that ogre eats us?" the cabbages asked the magpie.

"What a question!" the magpie cackled, almost toppling over his hopping legs in a squall of dirty laughter: "You'll all go into him or one of his friends or family and then come out as a nasty, stinking poo!"

Poos? None of the cabbages had the least idea of what this meant, but they drew their leaves tight around them in disgust.

That night our cabbage could not sleep. Presently the full moon came sailing into the coal black sky and its light-fingered rays splashed upon the earth and upon our cabbage who suddenly felt plucked free from its roots and fears. It was floating away now, our plump cabbage. And as it rose it seemed to turn into a round and green bubble. Up and up it floated as light as a feather on the wings of the wind. Wings? Did I say wings? But look, just look at what is happening to this round green bubble of a cabbage! Wings are growing from it! Out of that bubble has appeared a giant cabbage white butterfly with its huge white wings. One wing is Sheehee and the other is Heeshee, beating the air in perfect cabbage harmony.

And I think if you are very lucky, one day as
you gaze at the night sky, you will see our
cabbage. Sheehee will be one wing, Heeshee
the other, flying from star to star, as a
butterfly flies from flower to flower, free and
happy for evermore…

**And as for you, dream away for one
day your dreams too, may come true!**

www.ingramcontent.com/pod-product-compliance
Lightning Source LLC
Chambersburg PA
CBHW041542260326
41914CB00015B/1518